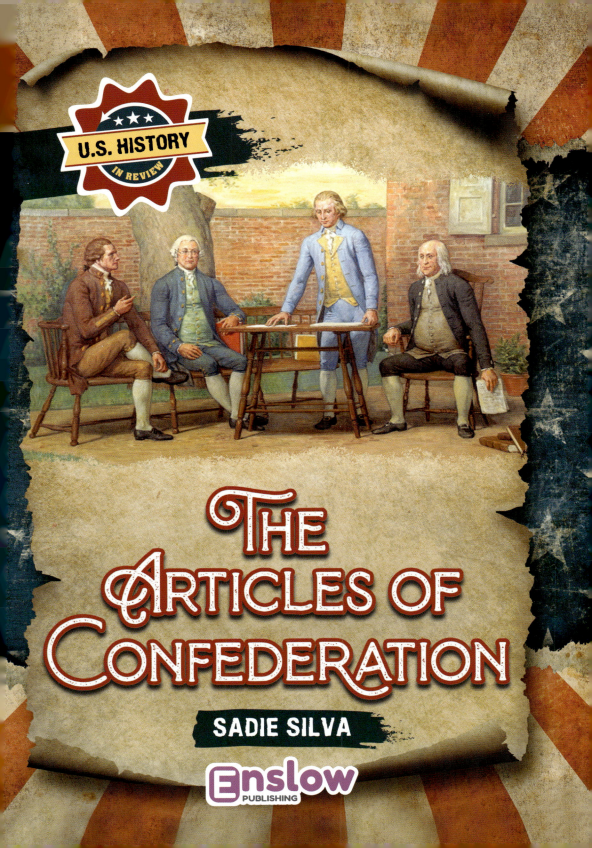

Please visit our website, www.enslow.com. For a free color catalog of all our high-quality books, call toll free 1-800-398-2504 or fax 1-877-980-4454.

Library of Congress Cataloging-in-Publication Data
Names: Silva, Sadie, author.
Title: The Articles of Confederation / Sadie Silva.
Description: Buffalo : Enslow Publishing, 2023. | Series: U.s. history in review | Includes index.
Identifiers: LCCN 2022020895 (print) | LCCN 2022020896 (ebook) | ISBN 9781978529045 (library binding) | ISBN 9781978529021 (paperback) | ISBN 9781978529052 (ebook)
Subjects: LCSH: United States. Articles of Confederation–Juvenile literature. | Constitutional history–United States–Juvenile literature. | United States–Politics and government–History–Juvenile literature.
Classification: LCC KF4508 .S55 2023 (print) | LCC KF4508 (ebook) | DDC 342.7302/9–dc23/eng/20220630
LC record available at https://lccn.loc.gov/2022020895
LC ebook record available at https://lccn.loc.gov/2022020896

Published in 2023 by
Enslow Publishing
2544 Clinton Street
Buffalo, NY 14224

Copyright © 2023 Enslow Publishing

Portions of this work were originally authored by Bray Jacobson and published as *The Articles of Confederation*. All new material in this edition authored by Sadie Silva.

Designer: Leslie Taylor
Editor: Caitlin McAneney

Photo credits: Cover https://commons.wikimedia.org/wiki/File:Congress_voting_independence.jpg; series art (grunge flag) Andrey Kuzmin/Shutterstock.com; series art (stamp icon) Stocker_team/Shutterstock.com; series art (font) santstock/Shutterstock.com; p. 5 Niday Picture Library/Alamy.com; p. 7 Jeffrey M. Frank/Shutterstock.com; p. 8 https://commons.wikimedia.org/wiki/File:Articles_of_Confederation_and_Perpetual_Union_between_the_states_of_New_Hampshire_..._LCCN2005696018.tif; p. 9 Everett Collection/Shutterstock.com; p. 11 North Wind Picture Archives/Alamy.com; p. 13 Niday Picture Library/Alamy.com; p. 15 https://commons.wikimedia.org/wiki/File:Articles_of_Confederation_(3695598804).jpg; p. 17 artnana/Shutterstock.com; p. 19 vkilikov/Shutterstock.com; p. 21 Bill Morson/Shutterstock.com; p. 23 Lonnie Paulson/Shutterstock.com; p. 25 ttps://commons.wikimedia.org/wiki/File:Ordinance2_of_1787.jpg; p. 27 (PA currency) https://commons.wikimedia.org/wiki/File:Currency,_Continental,_1776.jpg; p. 27 (Vermont currency) https://commons.wikimedia.org/wiki/File:US-Colonial_(VT-4)-Vermont-Feb_1781_OBV.jpg; p. 27 (NJ currency) Morphart Creation/Shutterstock.com; p. 29 Everett Collection/Shutterstock.com.

All rights reserved. No part of this book may be reproduced in any form without permission in writing from the publisher, except by a reviewer.

Printed in the United States of America

CPSIA compliance information: Batch #CWENS23: For further information, contact Enslow Publishing at 1-800-398-2504.

Find us on

Colonial Unrest	4
Ideas for the Future	6
Making a Plan	10
The Original Articles	12
Ready and Ratified	14
A Look at the Articles	16
Issues with the Articles	24
A New Constitution	28
Timeline	30
Glossary	31
For More Information	32
Index	32

Words in the glossary appear in **bold** the first time they are used in the text.

Colonial Unrest

After 150 years of peace in the British **colonies** of North America, colonists were getting upset. Many felt Great Britain was taxing and treating them unfairly. They wanted more say in British government. So, the First Continental Congress met in Philadelphia, Pennsylvania, in September 1774.

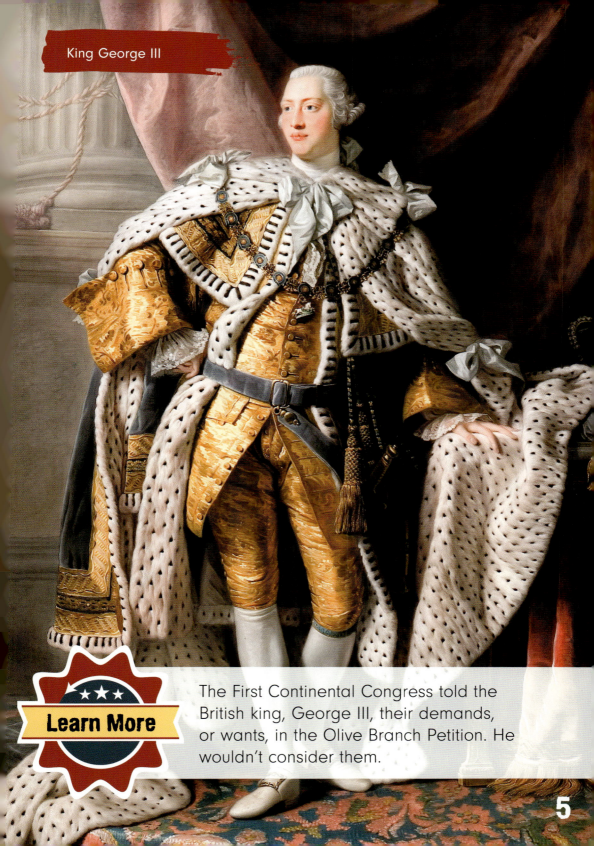

King George III

Learn More

The First Continental Congress told the British king, George III, their demands, or wants, in the Olive Branch Petition. He wouldn't consider them.

Ideas for the Future

In April 1775, the Battles of Lexington and Concord became the first of the **American Revolution**. The next month, the Second Continental Congress met at Independence Hall in Philadelphia. Some **representatives** wanted to **declare** independence, or freedom. All American colonies would have to join together under one government.

Independence Hall
Philadelphia, Pennsylvania

Learn More

Benjamin Franklin had presented the Albany Plan in 1754. The Albany Plan said the colonies would govern themselves, but still answer to the British king.

The Continental Congress was the voice of the colonies to Great Britain during the American Revolution. On July 21, 1775, Benjamin Franklin presented a new document to set up an independent government.

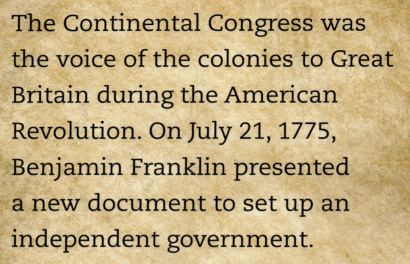

It was called the "Articles of Confederation and Perpetual Union."

Benjamin Franklin

Learn More

The Continental Congress talked about Franklin's document—but didn't **ratify** it. Franklin's was a major step toward the colonies' future government.

Making a Plan

Richard Henry Lee presented his own plan for independence on June 7, 1776. The Lee **Resolution** suggested that three **documents** be written. These were a "plan of confederation," a plan to make **alliances** with other countries, and a declaration of independence.

Richard Henry Lee

Learn More

A confederation is a group of people or states that support each other and act together. The colonies had many differences but had to act as one.

The Original Articles

A committee, or group, was formed to write the plan for confederation. John Dickinson of Pennsylvania wrote a **draft** of the Articles of Confederation. He presented it on July 12, 1776. It was clear many changes would need to be made.

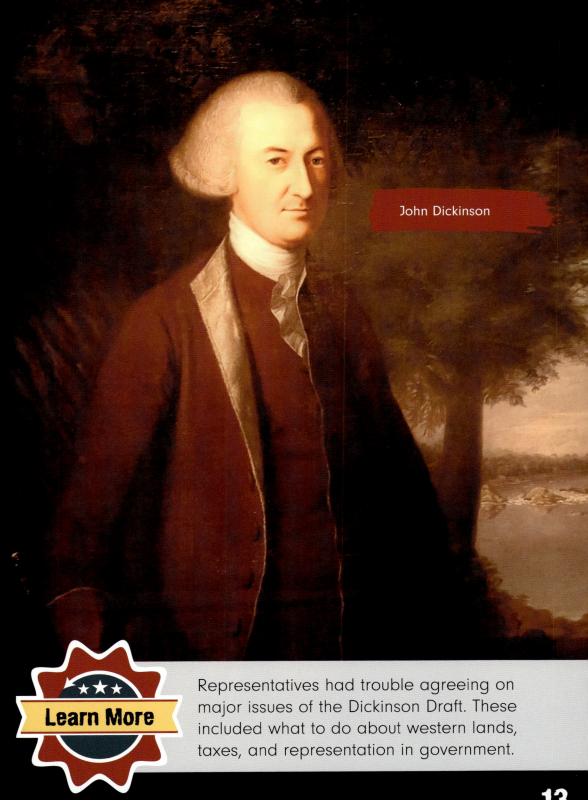

John Dickinson

Learn More

Representatives had trouble agreeing on major issues of the Dickinson Draft. These included what to do about western lands, taxes, and representation in government.

Ready and Ratified

In the Dickinson Draft, more power was held by the central, or national, government. In the final document, states had more power than the central government. On November 15, 1777, the Articles of Confederation was officially ratified by the Congress.

Articles of Confederation

Learn More

All 13 colony-states had to ratify the Articles of Confederation as well. Maryland didn't ratify the document until 1781!

A Look at the Articles

The United States was given its name in Article 1. Article 2 gave powers not with the central government to states. Article 3 said the states would unite against enemies. Article 4 said people could travel between the states freely, with limits for people who had broken the law.

Learn More

The Articles of Confederation included 13 articles, or parts. It established a "league of friendship" between the 13 states.

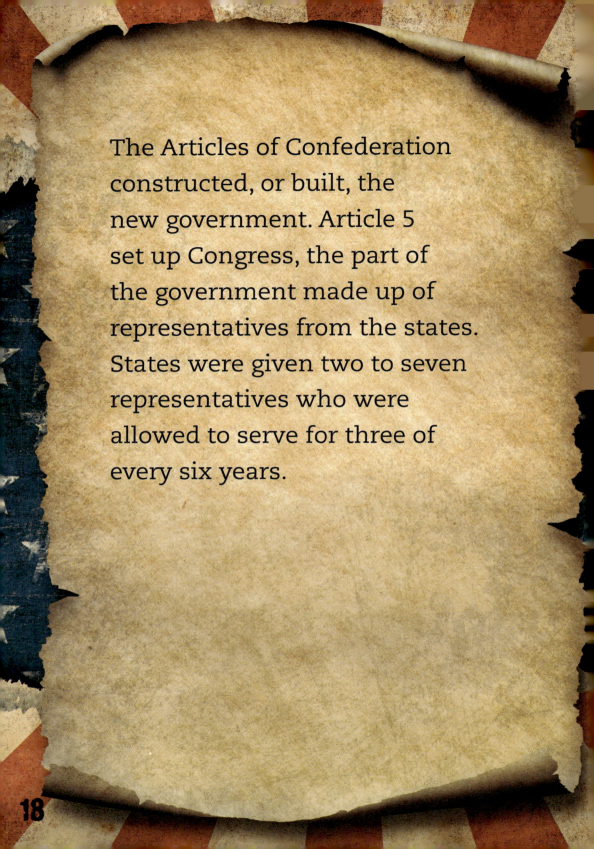

The Articles of Confederation constructed, or built, the new government. Article 5 set up Congress, the part of the government made up of representatives from the states. States were given two to seven representatives who were allowed to serve for three of every six years.

Learn More

A state's representatives would vote together, giving each state one vote in Congress.

Continental Congress

States had a lot of power under the Articles of Confederation. However, they still had some limits. Article 6 said they couldn't form alliances without Congress's approval or raise **permanent** armed forces. Article 8 created a way for the government to make money through state taxes.

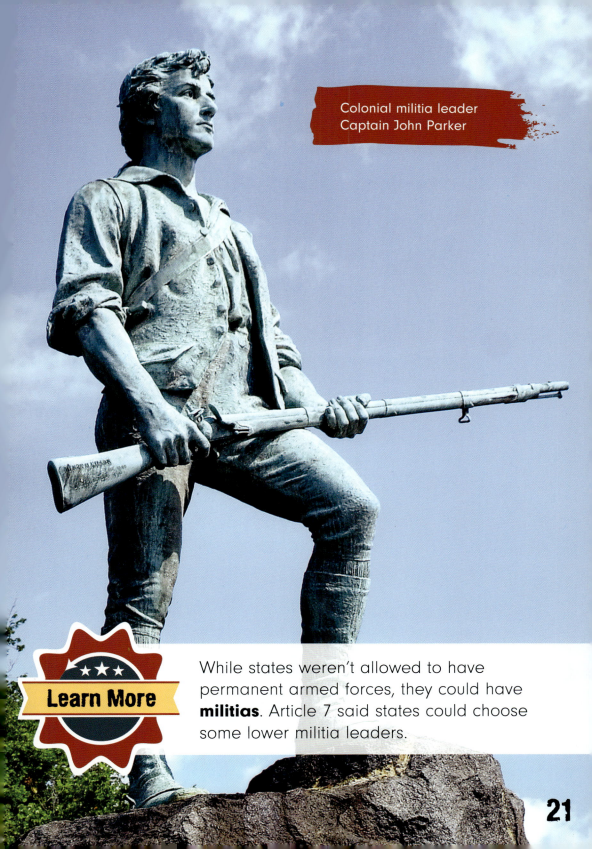

Colonial militia leader Captain John Parker

Learn More

While states weren't allowed to have permanent armed forces, they could have **militias**. Article 7 said states could choose some lower militia leaders.

21

Article 9 gave Congress power to deal with issues with other countries and problems between states. Article 10 said a Committee of States could make decisions when Congress wasn't meeting. Article 11 made adding new states possible. Article 12 handled war debts, or money owed to other countries.

Vermont, first state to be added to the United States (1791)

Article 13 made the Articles of Confederation the top law of the land. However, if states ratified changes, the document could be amended, or changed.

Issues with the Articles

The Articles of Confederation were a good starting point for the nation. However, issues soon arose. The Articles of Confederation gave too much power to the states. That's partly because many colonists felt more loyal to their state than the new country.

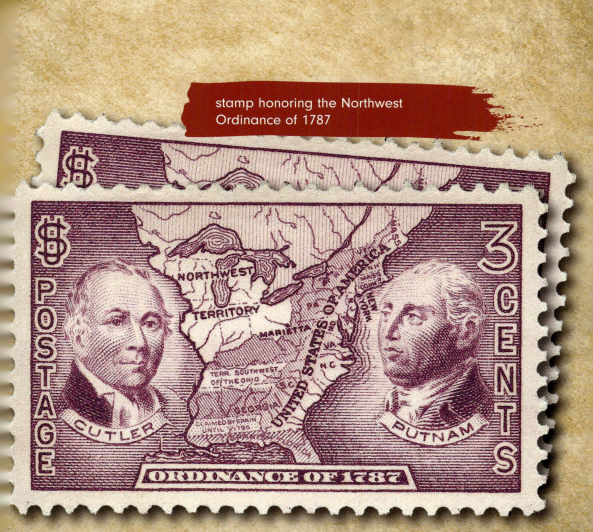

stamp honoring the Northwest Ordinance of 1787

Congress had one major success under the Articles of Confederation. It passed the Northwest Ordinance in 1787, which set up how western lands could become states.

25

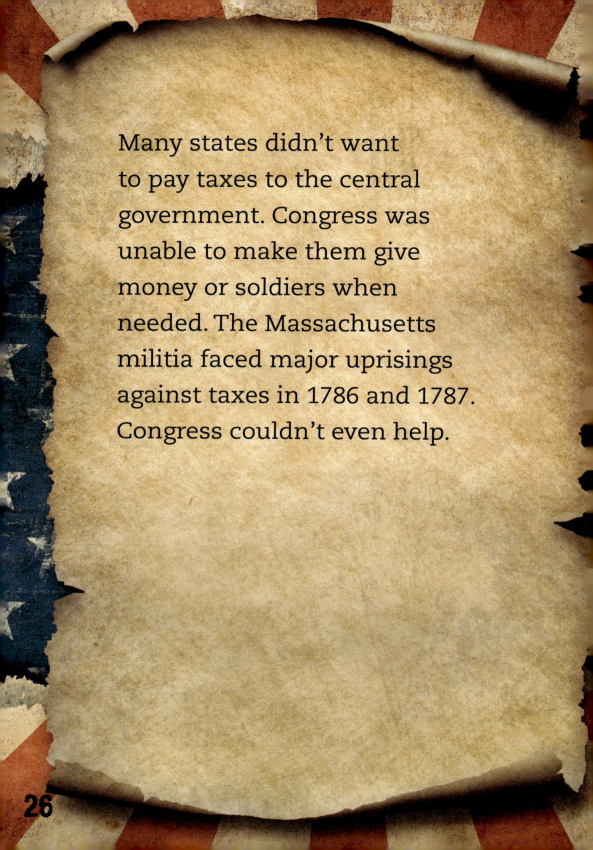

Many states didn't want to pay taxes to the central government. Congress was unable to make them give money or soldiers when needed. The Massachusetts militia faced major uprisings against taxes in 1786 and 1787. Congress couldn't even help.

Learn More

Each state had its own **currency,** or money, making trade between states hard. Federal money wasn't worth much.

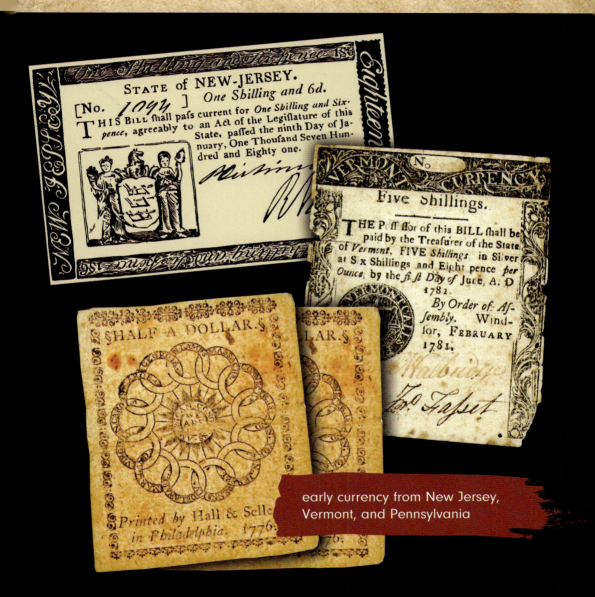

early currency from New Jersey, Vermont, and Pennsylvania

A New Constitution

In 1787, representatives from the states met to work out the Articles' problems. Instead, they chose to write a whole new document, the U.S. Constitution. It gave more power to the central government. The Articles of Confederation had served its purpose. Its chapter in U.S. history came to an end.

Constitutional Convention

The meeting of representatives to create the new constitution was called the Constitutional **Convention**. The U.S. Constitution went into effect in 1789.

Timeline

1754
Benjamin Franklin presents the Albany Plan.

September 5, 1774
The First Continental Congress meets in Philadelphia, Pennsylvania.

April 19, 1775
The American Revolution begins with the Battles of Lexington and Concord.

May 5, 1775
The Second Continental Congress begins.

July 21, 1775
Benjamin Franklin presents the "Articles of Confederation and Perpetual Union."

June 7, 1776
Richard Henry Lee presents a plan for confederation.

July 12, 1776
John Dickinson presents his draft of the Articles of Confederation to Congress.

November 15, 1777
The Articles of Confederation is officially ratified by Congress.

January 30, 1781
Maryland is the last state to ratify the Articles of Confederation.

July 13, 1787
Congress passes the Northwest Ordinance.

March 4, 1789
The U.S. Constitution replaces the Articles of Confederation.

Glossary

alliance: An agreement between two or more groups to work together.

American Revolution: The war in which the colonies won their freedom from England.

colony: A piece of land under the control of another country.

convention: A gathering of people who have a common interest or purpose.

declare: To state or announce.

document: A formal piece of writing.

draft: An early form of a document.

militia: A group of people who only fight when needed.

permanent: Unable to be removed.

ratify: To give formal approval to something.

representative: One who stands for a group of people.

resolution: An official statement of purpose voted on by a group.

For More Information

Books

Carr, Aaron. *Independence Hall*. New York, NY: AV2, 2022.

Keppeler, Jill. *Team Time Machine Crashes the Constitutional Convention*. New York, NY: Gareth Stevens Publishing, 2021.

Website

American Revolution: Articles of Confederation
www.ducksters.com/history/american_revolution/articles_of_confederation.php
Explore more interesting facts about the Articles of Confederation.

Publisher's note to educators and parents: Our editors have carefully reviewed these websites to ensure that they are suitable for students. Many websites change frequently, however, and we cannot guarantee that a site's future contents will continue to meet our high standards of quality and educational value. Be advised that students should be closely supervised whenever they access the internet.

Index

alliances, 10, 20
central government, 14, 16, 26, 28
Constitutional Convention, 29
currency, 27
Dickinson, John, 12, 13
First Continental Congress, 4, 5
Franklin, Benjamin, 7, 8, 9
Independence Hall, 6, 7
Lee, Richard Henry, 10, 11
Northwest Ordinance, 25
Olive Branch Petition, 5
Second Continental Congress, 6, 8, 9